THE WORLD OF...

Geography
Revision

Lynn Huggins-Cooper

Good day. I'm Sir Ralph Witherbottom. I'm an accomplished inventor, a dashing discoverer and an enthusiastic entrepreneur.

Hi! I'm Isabella Witherbottom – my friends call me Izzy. I'm Sir Ralph's daughter and I like to keep him on his toes!

And they both keep me on my toes! How do you do? I'm Max, the butler, at your service.

Woof! I'm Spotless – aptly named, as you can see. I'm the family's loyal dog.

Contents

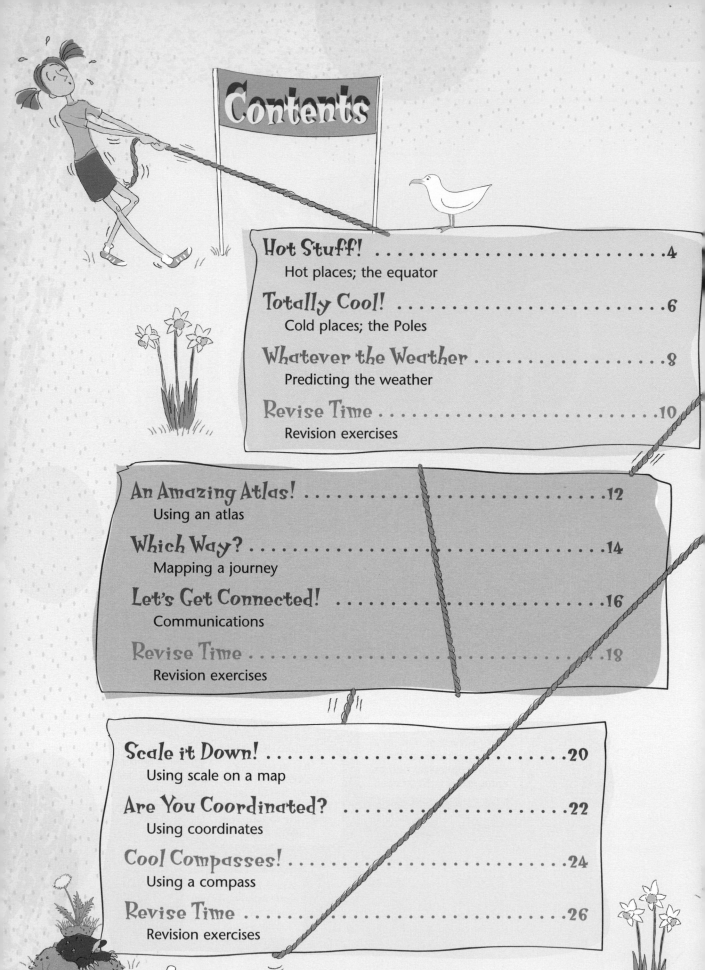

Hot Stuff!

Isabella is looking at a **globe** in Sir Ralph Witherbottom's study.

"It's funny looking at all the countries in the world on a little ball like this, Max! It's harder to understand than a flat map," said Isabella.

"That's true, Izzy, but then the world is round, after all!" said Max, the butler.

Isabella pulled an **atlas** down off the shelf. "I suppose so. The countries look so different on a map though. Why is that?"

"Well, when you try to draw a flat map of the round world, some parts get kind of stretched out of shape," said Max.

"What's this thick line round the middle of the globe, Max?" asked Isabella.

"It's the **equator**. It's an imaginary line halfway between the two poles. The two poles are found at the top and bottom of a globe," said Max. "The top half of the world is called the northern **hemisphere** and the bottom half is called the southern hemisphere. Around the equator, countries are very hot. Tropical **rainforests** are found around the area and they are hot and damp all year round. Here's the North Pole at the top of the world and here's the South Pole at the bottom."

"Max, that can't be the North Pole!" laughed Isabella.

"Why ever not, Izzy?" asked Max, looking puzzled.

"Because I can't see Santa's house!" laughed Isabella, spinning the globe.

Perhaps Santa's on holiday somewhere near the equator!

4

Label the map

Label these things on the map:

Equator   Northern Hemisphere   Southern Hemisphere
North Pole   South Pole

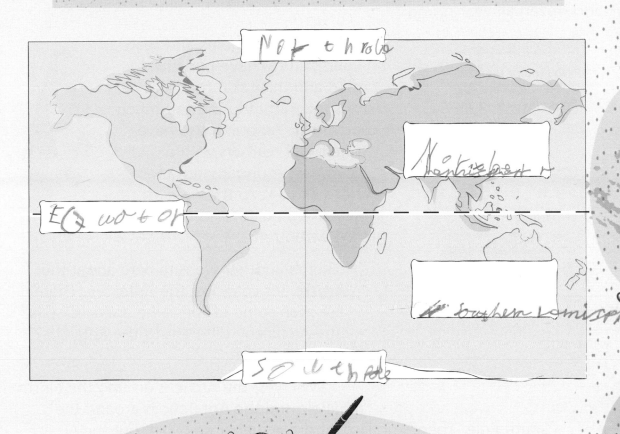

Not th role

Northishere

EQ wot or

southern hemisphere

south Pole

Top Tips

Look at a globe and a world map side by side. Can you see any differences in the shape of the countries?

Did you know?

Take an orange out of the fruit bowl and peel it. It is nearly impossible to make the orange skin into a flat picture that shows what an orange looks like. It is a little like that for map makers. The shape of countries changes a little as the round shape is flattened to draw a map on a page.

Totally Cool!

Isabella looked on the Internet to find out about the North and South Poles.

"Wow, dad, look at these animals – blue whales, seals, penguins… This site about the **Antarctic** says these creatures have a protective layer of fat that keeps them warm despite the freezing conditions. The Antarctic is very cold and frozen all year round."

"Yes, Izzy. The penguins and seals in your pictures have **compact** bodies and thick skin too. This stops them from losing too much body heat. Penguins also have waterproof feathers with a downy layer underneath that traps air to keep them warm, just like a quilt!" said Sir Ralph Witherbottom.

> No land at the North Pole? So where does Santa live – on a boat?

"There's another website here about the **Arctic**. It's cold, like the Antarctic. There are even some of the same animals. So is the Arctic any different to the Antarctic?" asked Isabella.

"Well, yes; the Arctic is around the North Pole and the Antarctic is around the South Pole. There's no land at the actual North Pole, but the Arctic Ocean is brimming with life. There's a lot of cold, windy land in the Arctic Circle though, including parts of Asia, Europe and North America. The land is called **tundra**," said Sir Ralph.

"It says on this site that there's permanently frozen soil, called **permafrost**. In the summer, there are very long periods of light and in winter there are long periods of darkness. The animals that live there, such as the Arctic fox and the ermine, have fur that gets thicker and turns white for **camouflage** in the snow. Some animals **hibernate** and others **migrate** to escape the cold," said Isabella.

"And who can blame them, Izzy? I'd like to do that in the winter too!" laughed Sir Ralph.

Word scramble

Unscramble these words to do with the North and South Poles.

1 untard   _tundra_

2 leas   _seal_

3 eath   _heat_

4 pelo   _pole_

5 thorn   _north_

6 thous   _south_

7 yiwnd   _windy_

8 ticrac   _arctic_

Top Tips

Do an Internet search to see how many other animals change colour in winter.

Did you know?

The South Pole is the coldest place on earth. The lowest temperature ever recorded was at the South Pole – a bitterly cold –128.6°F (–88.0°C)! Strangely, Antarctica is a very dry place, like a frozen desert! There is less **precipitation** than in the Sahara Desert. To make it even weirder, 70% of the world's fresh water is stored in the South Pole region – as ice!

Whatever the Weather

Isabella has decided to set up a **weather station** in the garden. Sir Ralph Witherbottom has brought along some things to help her.

"All set! I've made a **rain gauge** from a bottle to see how much rain falls, a weather vane to show the wind direction and Max has lent me his greenhouse **thermometer** to check temperatures," said Isabella.

"Excellent! I've got a few things you can use to help predict the weather, too! Here's a **barometer**. It measures **atmospheric pressure**. This can help you to work out if there's going to be rain," said Sir Ralph.

"That's great, dad! What are these funny things though?" asked Isabella.

"Well, these things have difficult names. This is an **anemometer**. It measures wind speed," said Sir Ralph. "And this odd thing is a **hygrometer**. It's used to measure humidity – which is the dampness in the air."

"I've got a journal to record the weather each day – and to write my predictions in!" said Isabella. "So now I'm all ready!"

I just need to know if it'll be dry and windy!

"When you've collected your data, Izzy, I'll help you to enter it onto the computer. We can make a **spreadsheet**, and then use the information to create charts and **graphs** to show your findings. Recording the information in this way will help you to see any patterns that appear in your weather findings, and that may help you to predict how the weather will change in the future!" said Sir Ralph.

What is it for?

Draw a line to join the name of the instrument to what it is used for.

1	Thermometer		To measure humidity.
2	Rain gauge		To measure temperature.
3	Weather vane		To record readings.
4	Barometer		To measure atmospheric pressure.
5	Anemometer		To measure rainfall.
6	Hygrometer		To measure wind speed.
7	Journal		To find wind direction.

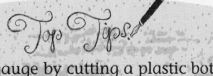

Top Tips!

Make a rain gauge by cutting a plastic bottle in half.
Using the bottom of the bottle, mark the side in
centimetres with a ruler and permanent marker pen.

Did you know?

The weather forecasts that we see on the television use similar instruments to the ones on this page – they are just more sensitive and are linked to computers. Satellite pictures are also used. These are photographs taken from space, which show different weather systems, such as clouds, as they move across different areas. Watch the weather forecast on TV and you will see them!'

Revise Time

1 **Fill in the missing words, using the words in the box.**

bottom equator South Pole rainforests North Pole northern

a Around the _____ countries are very hot.

b Tropical jungles called _____ are found around the equator.

c The top half of the world is called the _____ hemisphere.

d The _____ half of the world is called the southern hemisphere.

e The _____ is found at the top of a globe.

f The _____ is found at the bottom of a globe.

2 **Describe these things**

a Globe   _____

b Atlas   _____

c Equator   _____

d Southern hemisphere _____

e Northern hemisphere _____

f Rainforest   _____

3 **Fill in the missing letters.**

a P _ _ _ uin

b _ _ _ arctic

c A _ _ _ ic

d Perm _ _ _ _ st

e _ und _ _

f _ _ berna _ _

4 **Answer these questions about the poles.**

a What is 'permafrost'? _____

b Why do animals that live in the Antarctic have a thick layer of fat?

_____

c Name three continents found in the Arctic Circle.

_____

d Name two animals you might find at the North Pole.

_____

e Name two animals you might find at the South Pole.

_____

5 **Match the words to the meanings.**

a Graph   1 A measure of how hot or cold it is.

b Wind speed   2 Writing down, making notes, taking pictures, making drawings, etc. to show what has happened.

c Temperature   3 A way of recording measurements.

d Humid   4 Warm and damp.

e Recording   5 How fast the wind is travelling.

6 **Name three items you might find in a weather station and explain what they do.**

_____

_____

_____

An Amazing Atlas!

Max has given Isabella a **picture atlas** of her own and they are looking at it together.

"This is great, Max – thanks!" said Isabella.

"It's a special atlas, just for kids. It doesn't just have maps inside – it has pictures of things on the maps, to help you to learn about the countries," said Max.

"Look at this map of Europe, Max! I can see a picture of the TGV train, like the one we went on last year in France! There's a little person skiing on the map of Switzerland – and that big mountain is Mont Blanc!" said Isabella.

"Ah, yes – do you remember the postcard I sent you from Mont Blanc a few years ago, with a picture of the little **chamois** antelopes that are found on the peaks in summer? Such lovely little animals!" Max smiled.

"I do! Look – there's Holland and a picture of **The Hague**. Dad's been there. He said the parliament building is lovely, but not half as impressive as our Houses of Parliament!" said Isabella.

"Look – there's Spain, with an orange tree near Valencia. If you look in the greengrocer's or the supermarket, you'll see lots of oranges with stickers on that say 'Spain' or even 'Valencia'. Valencia produces some of Spain's sweetest oranges," said Max.

"Here's Italy, with a picture of the Leaning Tower of Pisa, and there's the Pope's palace – **the Vatican** – that's in Rome. There's a lovely cheesy pizza, too... this is all making me hungry, Max! I don't suppose there's any chance of some lunch, is there?"

Of course, she didn't ask for a healthy orange...!

1025
1020
1015
1011

0

Draw the items

Draw items on the map for each country. You may use the things that Isabella and Max talked about or think of new things yourself!

Top Tips!

Look at the Dorling Kindersley Picture Atlas by Anita Ganeri and Chris Oxlade – it is full of great information and beautiful maps.

Did you know?

A picture atlas gives you information not just about where countries are in the world, but also about what each country is like physically (i.e. whether it has mountains, jungles or deserts); about the people and animals that live there; what famous buildings there are and perhaps even what food is traditional!

500

Which Way?

Isabella has to draw a map of her journey to school for her geography homework. She has taken Spotless for a walk so she can check her **route**.

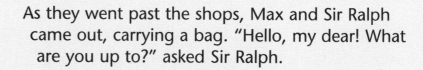

"Right, boy – let's walk from home to school. I've brought a pencil and a sketch pad, so I can roughly draw out my map," said Isabella.

They walked down the road and turned left. "I've sketched Livingstone Road on the map, and I'm going to put the station on it too, because it's a **landmark**, Spotless. That means it's something you can look out for to help you find your way," she said.

They walked down the road, past the war memorial. Isabella marked it on the map. Then she drew Church Road and marked the bus stops at the side of the road.

As they went past the shops, Max and Sir Ralph came out, carrying a bag. "Hello, my dear! What are you up to?" asked Sir Ralph.

"I'm drawing a map of my route to school for homework. Once I get round the corner, I'll be finished, because I'll be in front of the school gates!" she said.

"We'll come along too," said Max, "because we were just going to ask you – and Spotless of course – if you'd like to come for a picnic in the park. We've just bought sandwiches in the baker's."

"Lovely! Homework finished already – and before tea!" laughed Isabella.

"I think that's a first, Izzy!" said Sir Ralph.

Draw a map

Draw a map of your own route to school in the box below. Don't forget to add landmarks!

Top Tips

You can check the map you drew against a street map of your town to see if it is accurate.

Did you know?

Maps help people to find their way to places. They are usually drawn to **scale**. That means that although everything on the map is smaller than in real life, the things that appear on it are still in **proportion** to one another. A large building, such as a school, will be much bigger than a house, for example.

500

Let's Get Connected!

Dear Izzy,
How are you?

I have been on holiday with my family. We had a nice time.

Isabella got a letter from her pen pal, Luisa. Luisa lives in Essen, in Germany. "Look, dad! I got a letter from Luisa. She's been on holiday with her family, but now she's home again. She sent a picture too…isn't her house lovely?" said Isabella.

"It is, Izzy, and you'll get a chance to see it for yourself in the summer, when you go on your **exchange trip**!" said Sir Ralph.

"I must write straight back to her," said Isabella, "but it takes so long – writing the letter, putting it in an envelope, going to the post office to send it air mail – and then it takes ages to get to Germany!"

"Well, why don't you email Luisa instead? It's very quick and easy and gets to its destination virtually instantly! What more could you ask of a method of **communication**?" said Sir Ralph.

"It even saves trees, Izzy, which should appeal to a nature-loving girl like you!" laughed Max.

"What a great idea! Mr Grimes, our German teacher, has set up a website 'twinning' our school with Luisa's school in Essen. It has information comparing the two schools – and the towns, too!" said Isabella.

"You can even send photos of your own, Izzy, by attaching photos taken with your digital camera to your email," said Max. "I can help you to load them onto the computer later."

"Excellent! I can't wait to get started!" said Isabella happily. "The Internet makes the world seem smaller, doesn't it?"

Maybe I'll email the p shop. 'Please send 3 bones…2 chew toys..

1025
1020
1015
1011

0

Better than a letter

Write an email to a friend explaining why emails are a better way to keep in touch than letters.

in　　send　　trash　　draft

To

___

Top Tips!

Have a look at Kidlink, a great international Internet-based organisation that allows children around the world to keep in touch.
http://www.kidlink.org/

Did you know?

People sometimes say that communication has made the world smaller. They obviously don't mean physically smaller – just that increased communications have made it easier to stay in touch! You can now email your friend across the other side of the world in seconds. In the past, before the Internet or telephones were invented, people had to wait weeks for a letter to be delivered, often by boat!

Revise Time

1 Match the item to the correct country with a line.

a France **b** Spain **c** Italy **d** Switzerland

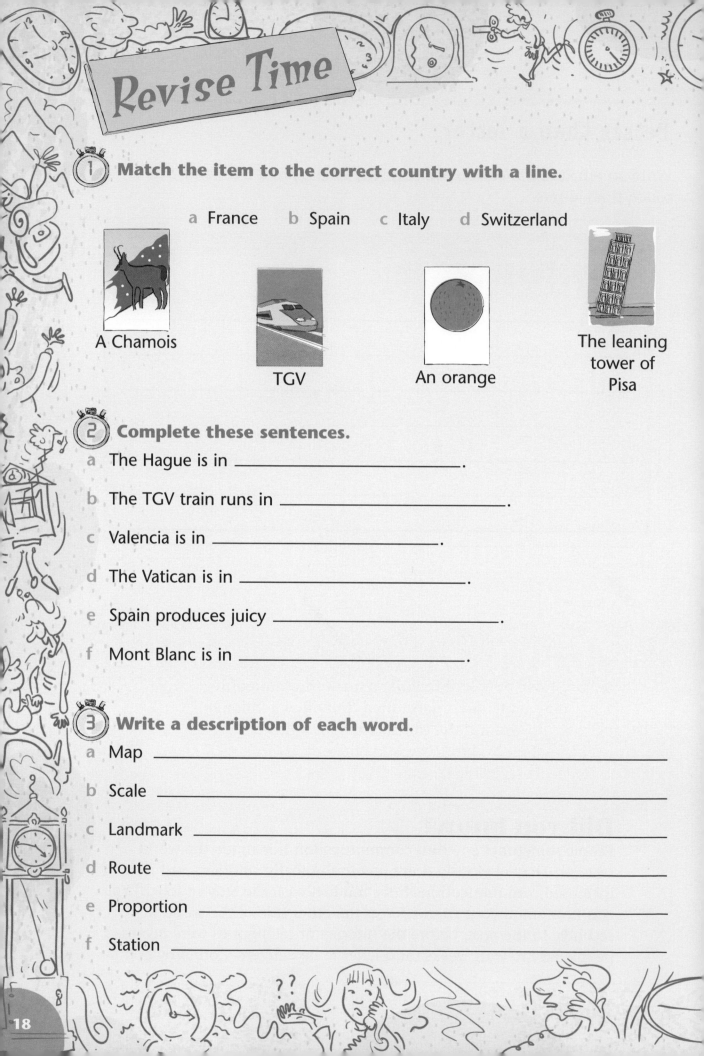

A Chamois

TGV

An orange

The leaning tower of Pisa

2 Complete these sentences.

a The Hague is in _____.

b The TGV train runs in _____.

c Valencia is in _____.

d The Vatican is in _____.

e Spain produces juicy _____.

f Mont Blanc is in _____.

3 Write a description of each word.

a Map _____

b Scale _____

c Landmark _____

d Route _____

e Proportion _____

f Station _____

4 Fill in the missing letters.

a Pr _ por _ ion

b Jou _ _ ey

c _ and _ ark

d R _ _ d

e _ out _

f M _ _

5 Join the jumbled words to their correct spelling with a line.

a rai imal   internet

b teirnten   air mail

c fionmtanori   information

d meali   photos

e cmmonucitaoni   communication

f hptoos   email

6 True or false? Write 'T' for true or 'F' for false in the boxes.

a You send an email over the Internet.

b You send an email through the post.

c It is faster to send a letter than an email.

d It is faster to send an email than a letter.

e The Internet makes the world seem smaller.

f The Internet makes the world seem larger.

Scale it Down!

Isabella is looking at a map of the local countryside. She has asked Sir Ralph to take her walking at the weekend and he has asked her to plan the route.

"This map is quite hard to understand, Max. I can't work out how far some of these routes are, and you know if I plan a route, dad will expect us to walk it – all of it – however far it is!" said Isabella.

"Well, Izzy, it's easy when you know how! The map has a **scale**. That means a certain distance on the map represents a certain distance on the ground. Let me look at your map," said Max.

"Here, Max. What does that box at the bottom of the page mean?" asked Isabella.

"It's called the **legend box**, Izzy. The box explains the **symbols** used on the map and gives other information about the map. These numbers here show the scale," said Max.

A legend? They must be talking about me...

Isabella looked at the numbers. They said 1:100,000.

"What do the numbers mean, Max?" asked Isabella.

"It means for every centimetre you can measure on the map, there are 100,000 centimetres (1 kilometre) in real life.

"The scale can also be written in words. It could say: 'One centimetre equals one kilometre' or it could be shown as a line, like this," said Max, showing Isabella another map with a drawn scale.

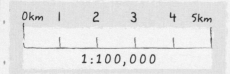

"Well, I think all these scales are a pain!" complained Isabella.

"True, but better that maps are drawn to scale rather than drawn actual size – or they'd be far too big to carry!" laughed Max.

Use the scale

Use the scale 1:100,000 and a ruler to answer the questions.

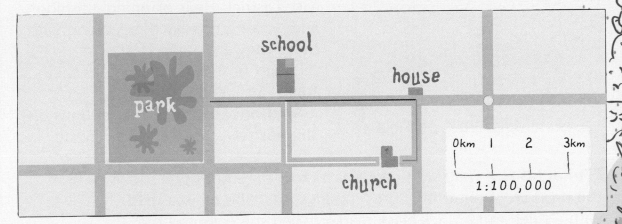

1 How far is it to walk from the house to the school? _____

2 How far is it to walk from the church to the house? _____

3 How far is it to walk from the church to the school? _____

4 How far is it to walk from the school to the park? _____

5 How far is it to walk from the house to the park? _____

6 How far is it to walk from the park to the church? _____

Top Tips

Look at different maps to see what particular type
of scale the mapmaker has chosen to use.

Did you know?

People who draw maps talk about large-scale and small-scale maps.
Large-scale maps show a small area with lots of detail. You would be
likely to make a small-scale map if you are planning your route to
school. Small-scale maps show larger areas without much detail.

Are You Coordinated?

Sir Ralph is looking at a map of the Lake District. He is planning a fishing and walking holiday there, along with Max. They are going to stay in different hostels each night, as they travel. Sir Ralph is using **coordinates** to find the positions of the hostels, so he can plot a route.

"I'm drawing a map with coordinates too, dad, but mine shows the position of pirate treasure!" said Isabella. She drew a **grid** with a ruler and a thick black marker. Then she coloured the background, drawing the sea – complete with a sea monster! She used a green felt pen to draw an island, with a big, erupting volcano, a jungle and a lake full of crocodiles!

She marked her grid with letters up the side and numbers along the bottom.

"Look, Max! The grid helps you to find all the things I've drawn on my map! If I tell you to go to G2, what can you see?" asked Isabella.

"A great big, scary sea serpent! I wouldn't like to meet one of those, Izzy! There's the volcano at B6...and the lake at D3...this is an excellent map, Izzy. It's so easy to find things!" said Max.

> Am I coordinated, Izzy?

"It's a little like my map, Izzy," said Sir Ralph. "But we don't have letters and numbers – we have two sets of numbers – but we use the grid in the same way. The correct set of **grid reference** numbers can tell you where to find anything on this map."

"I just hope there aren't any sea serpents in the lakes!" laughed Max.

Mark it out

Draw the things on the map in the correct place.

1 Treasure chest at B5

2 Skull and crossbones at D4

3 Ruined temple at F6

4 Well at C3

5 Ship at F2

6 Swamp at A8

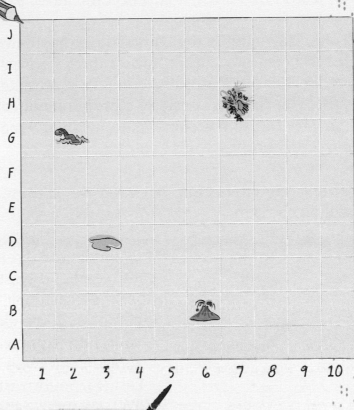

Top Tips

Have a go at making your own map with a grid.
You could even use it for a treasure hunting game!

Did you know?

Ordnance Survey maps are covered in blue grid lines. They help you to find any **location** on the map, if you have the grid reference. Four-figure grid references (such as 3421) are easy to read. The first two numbers match one of the vertical lines on the map's grid and the second two numbers match a horizontal line. Trace along the two lines until they cross. The box you want is the one above and to the right of this point.

Cool Compasses!

Sir Ralph has given Isabella her own **compass**, so she can learn how to use it and become a real explorer!

"Look, Izzy – this is the compass needle. It always points to the **magnetic North** Pole. Inside the compass there's a small magnet attached to the needle. The magnet in the compass is attracted to the magnetic pull of the earth. The compass needle points in one direction, towards the North Pole – so we can use the compass to help us to read a map. Clever, isn't it?" said Sir Ralph.

"That's very interesting, but what are all these letters round the edge for?" asked Isabella.

"Those show the directions, Izzy. Apart from north, south, east and west, there are directions in between each pair, as you go round the compass. These eight compass points read round the compass, starting from the top and moving clockwise – North (N), North east (NE), East (E), South east (SE), South (S), South west (SW), West (W), and North west (NW)," said Sir Ralph.

> Izzy could find her way to the sweet shop with her eyes shut – never mind the compass!

"You can even use sixteen compass points, Izzy, like North north west (NNW), but I think that might get a bit confusing right now!" said Max.

"Too right!" said Isabella. "I've only got as far as finding out that **Ordnance Survey maps** always have north marked at the top, and knowing that I mustn't keep anything that affects magnets in my pocket, even my front door key! I don't want to be baffled before I begin! Now, I'll use my trusty compass to guide me to the sweet shop…"

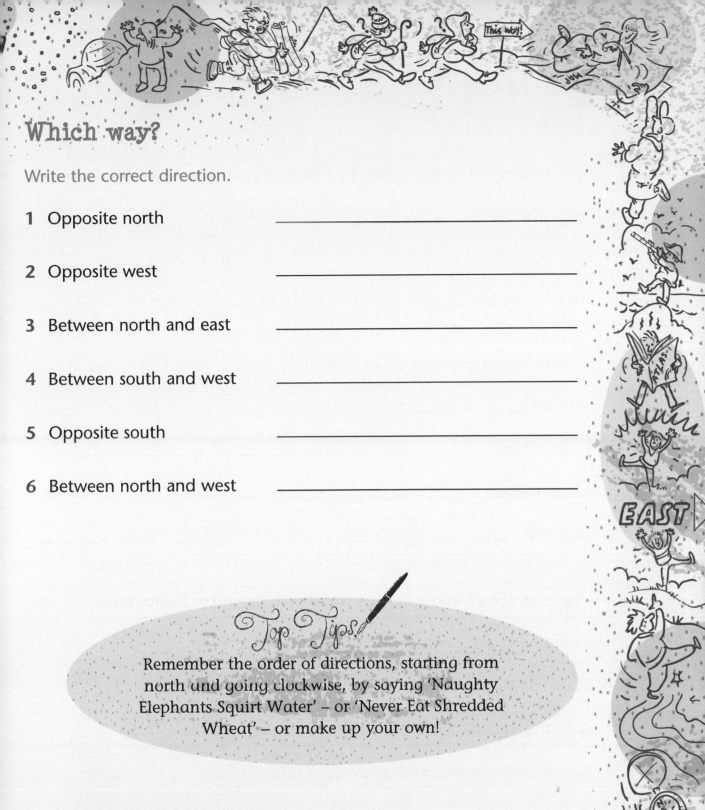

Which way?

Write the correct direction.

1 Opposite north _____

2 Opposite west _____

3 Between north and east _____

4 Between south and west _____

5 Opposite south _____

6 Between north and west _____

Top Tips

Remember the order of directions, starting from north and going clockwise, by saying 'Naughty Elephants Squirt Water' – or 'Never Eat Shredded Wheat' – or make up your own!

Did you know?

The current North Pole of the earth is actually a South Pole. Every few tens of thousands of years the earth's magnetic field flips! But don't worry; your compass was invented after the last flip, so it will still point north!

Revise Time

1 Fill in the missing letters to make words about scales.

a Sym _ o _

b Le _ e _ d

c Inf _ _ _ ati _ _

d Sca _ _

e R _ ut _

f Di _ _ _ nce

2 Write a description of each word.

a Symbol _____

b Legend box _____

c Measurement _____

d Distance _____

3 True or false? Write 'T' for true or 'F' for false in the boxes.

a Coordinates help people to find places on maps. ☐

b Coordinates do not help people to find places on maps. ☐

c A grid can be drawn with a ruler and pen. ☐

d A grid can be drawn with a ruler and rubber. ☐

e Grids can help you use numbers and letters to find
a position. ☐

f The correct set of grid reference numbers can tell you where to
find anything on a map. ☐

4 Draw these on the grid.

a A beetle at B4

b A ladybird at F2

c A worm at A6

d A snail at D3

F
E
D
C
B
A

1   2   3   4   5   6

5 Fill in the missing words.

a In a compass there is a small _____.

b The compass needle points in _____ direction.

c The needle always points to the _____ Pole.

d A compass helps us to find the correct _____.

e North east is between _____ and _____.

6 Draw the eight directions on the compass.

Magic Symbols!

Isabella and Max are driving through heavy traffic, on their way home. Isabella is bored, staring out of the window.

"Max, what does that sign mean?" asked Isabella.

"Do you mean the one with the big and small arrows going different ways? That means we have priority over traffic coming the other way, so it's our turn to go first through that part where the road narrows," answered Max.

"Hmm…so it's an important sign. Would you say the arrows are a **symbol** to let you know what to do, Max?" asked Isabella.

"Well, I would, but why are you asking all these questions, Izzy?" asked Max.

"Well, we're learning about symbols at school. My teacher, Mrs Carson, says that symbols are used to give us information quickly. She says that symbols on maps can show us where to find buildings, roads, rivers, caravan sites, places of interest…"

"Slow down, Izzy! Yes, symbols are very useful. Maps have a **key** to explain what the symbols stand for. Some are easy to guess, for example a caravan site is often a tiny caravan! A campsite may be shown by a tiny **tepee**, and a castle may be shown by a tiny castle symbol. I've even seen a duck standing for a nature reserve and a flower for gardens!"

Off to the youth hostel…!

"Wow! That's great!" said Isabella.

"It's very useful too, Izzy! Your dad and I looked for youth hostel symbols on an **Ordnance Survey map** when we were planning our hiking trip," said Max.

"Youth hostels! I thought they were places where youths stayed!" laughed Isabella.

Match them up

Draw a line between the symbol and its meaning.

1    Nature reserve

2    Campsite

3    Castle

4    Caravan site

5    Garden

Top Tips!

Look on an Ordnance Survey map and see if you
can work out what the symbols mean. Then look at
the key and see if you were right!

Did you know?

Youth hostels, run by the Youth Hostel Association, are cheap,
comfortable places to stay. They are not just for very young people!
Whatever your age, you can book a bed in a hostel. Some are in
purpose-built hostels, but others are in lovely old buildings such as
barns and old converted farmhouses.

Eye in the Sky

Sir Ralph was very excited. The post van had just delivered a large padded package.

"Careful, Spotless!" he said. "I know it's exciting, but if you keep running through my legs, I'll drop my parcel and the glass will break!"

As Sir Ralph opened the parcel, Isabella saw a large, framed photograph.

"What's this a photograph of, dad? I don't recognise it," said Isabella. "It looks like 'ant land'! The cars are so tiny! Look at the roundabout there, with all the roads leading off it. It looks like a big round spider!"

"It's our town, Izzy, and here's our house! This is an **aerial photograph**. They're taken from the sky, from planes or helicopters. Some are even taken by a satellite in space!" said Sir Ralph.

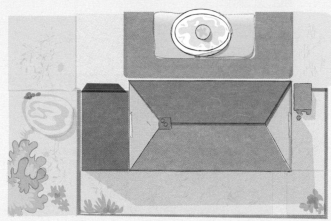

"Look here – can you see that open green area? That's the park. The big blue patch is the lake. Can you find the main road and the shopping centre?"

Another great aerial photo – of my kennel!

"Well, I know the main road will be wider than the others, and it's quite long, so I think it's that one there. The shopping centre would be bigger than the houses, so I need to look for something quite big... and I know the shopping centre is near the top end of the park... there it is!" exclaimed Isabella excitedly.

"Well done, Izzy! You've found it! One day I'd like to take aerial photos of my own. For now, though, I'll be happy to have this one in my study!" said Sir Ralph.

What can you see?

Look at the aerial photograph below and write the correct number in the box next to each place.

1   Park

2   Lake

3   Main road

4   Shopping centre

5   Roundabout

6   School and playground

Top Tips!

Ask at your local library – they may have an aerial photograph of your town!

Did you know?

Aerial photography was used during the Second World War by both sides. Small planes flew over Britain and Germany, taking aerial photographs. These photographs showed where the shipyards, factories, rivers and docks were. The information that was held in the photographs was used by the air force to find the targets they had to bomb during raids.

Travelling in Style!

Isabella is doing a project at school about transport. She is trying to think of all the different ways of travelling.

"Well, Spotless – apart from walking, we use the car the most. It's not just us, either! Most people in Britain travel by car. According to my teacher, 72% of households have at least one car – and many have more than one! Travelling by car, van or taxi is the most common sort of transport used in Britain. 85% of the miles travelled by passengers in Great Britain use these vehicles."

Max walked in with a pile of papers. "Here's some more information for your project, Izzy, about how goods and people are moved around the country. According to this, only 100 years ago, goods were moved around on trains and **canal barges**, but now goods are mainly moved on motorways and roads. You've seen all the big lorries and wagons thundering past on the motorway, haven't you?" said Max.

Sir Ralph came in with some photographs for Isabella to use in her project.

I rather fancy the train, myself…

"Don't forget that people travel in single decker and double decker buses! Then there are coaches, of course," said Sir Ralph.

"That's right – we used one for our school outing to the aquarium!" said Isabella. "There are taxis too – black cabs like the ones at the rank outside the station, as well as hire cars," said Isabella.

"Don't forget what's inside the station – the trains! Britain's **rail network** covers an amazing 16,659 kilometres. The underground railway in London – the 'tube' – is great for getting around quickly, too!" said Sir Ralph.

"Then there are planes and even bicycles! Wow, there really are so many different ways to travel! When can we try them all out?" laughed Isabella.

Which ones?

Circle the pictures which are types of transport.

   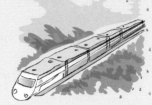

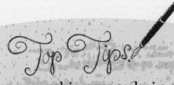

Top Tips
Do a survey, asking people in your class
how they got to school, to find out
which way was the most popular.

Did you know?

Heathrow and Gatwick Airports are the two main centres in England
for overseas flights. Heathrow Airport is one of the biggest airports in
the world! There are many smaller airports all over Britain, and
people fly on domestic flights, which means they fly from one part of
Britain to another, as well as international flights, which means
people fly from Britain to other countries.

Revise Time

1 **Answer these questions about map symbols.**

a   What is a key? _____

b   Why are map symbols useful? _____

c   What does a duck symbol on a map mean? _____

d   What is the symbol for a campsite? _____

e   What does a flower symbol on a map mean? _____

f   What is the symbol for a castle? _____

g   What does a caravan symbol on a map mean? _____

2 **Draw the symbols in the boxes.**

a   Caravan site

d   Castle

b   Campsite

e   Nature reserve

c   Garden

3 **Fill in the missing first and last letters of these words to do with maps.**

a   _ eria _   c   _ hoppin _   _ entr _   e   _ ouse _

b   _ hotograp _   d   _ oundabou _

34

4 Answer these questions.

a Where are aerial photographs taken from?

_____

b Why do things look so small in aerial photographs?

_____

c What might a green area on an aerial photograph be? _____

d What might a blue patch on an aerial photograph be? _____

5 Fill in the missing words. Use the words in the box to help you.

network   decker   cabs   tube   coaches   cars

a _____ are often used for school outings.

b The underground railway in London is called the _____.

c Black _____ are found at ranks.

d Hire _____ are similar to taxis.

e Britain's rail _____ covers 16,659 kilometres.

f You get double and single _____ buses.

6 Fill in the missing numbers, using the numbers in the box.

100   85   2   72   16,659

a _____ % of households in Britain have at least one car.

b _____ % of the miles travelled by passengers in Great Britain are by

car, van or taxi.

c The British rail network covers _____ kilometres.

d _____ years ago, goods were moved by trains and canal barges.

e Buses can have one or _____ decks.

Happy Holidays

Max was looking in a magazine, reading about the places people from Britain go on their holidays.

"It says here, Sir Ralph, that two thirds of all British people take their holidays in July and August. It's not so much that July and August are the most popular months for holidays – it's just that the children are on school holidays then!" said Max.

"It's certainly the most expensive time to book a holiday – you see the prices in the **brochures** shoot up during the school holidays!" grumbled Sir Ralph.

I'm ready!

"I remember when the traditional British holiday was to go to the seaside in this country, but now everybody seems to go **abroad**. Lots of people go to warm places, such as Spain and Portugal, but many people have skiing holidays in the snow, too," said Max.

Isabella came and sat at the table and looked over Max's shoulder.

"Wow! I didn't realise that so many people went on holiday!" said Isabella. "This magazine article says that in 2002, British people made 12.6 million visits to Spain, and 11.7 million visits to France! 3 million visits were made to Greece – we were there!"

"Yes Izzy, lots of people go on holiday and many of them go twice a year! Lots of British people take a winter holiday as well as a summer holiday and more people are now taking short breaks, sometimes just for the weekend, to European cities," said Sir Ralph.

"What a great idea, dad! When are we going?" Isabella laughed.

Heads and tails

Fill in the first two missing letters and the last two missing letters to make the words in the box.

| British | summer | brochure | school | holiday | winter |

1 _ _ lid _ _

2 _ _ mm _ _

3 _ _ nt _ _

4 _ _ ochu _ _

5 _ _ ho _ _

6 _ _ iti _ _

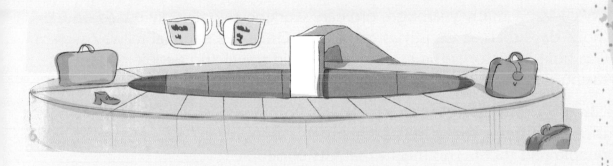

Top Tips

Collect some holiday brochures from a travel agent – and plan your 'dream' holiday!

Did you know?

Tourism can be a very important way for people in poor countries to earn money. Tourists take money on holiday to spend on food, drinks and souvenirs. Some people think that tourism is a bad thing though. They are worried that local people will lose their land and houses as big new hotels are built, and that the money spent will only go to rich people, such as restaurant and hotel owners.

Holiday History

Sir Ralph brought a box of black and white photographs into the room. They showed his family at the seaside when he was a little boy.

"These were great holidays! We went to Brighton, Blackpool, Scarborough and Bournemouth, and had a great time. We watched Punch and Judy shows, ate candyfloss and ice-cream, and crunched on candy rock. I loved to make sandcastles, while my parents sat in deckchairs nearby."

"You sound as though you had fun, dad! Very different to our holidays though, in Greece and Egypt and other countries far away! So how have holidays changed for people over the years?"

"Well, Izzy – many years ago, ordinary working people only rested on 'holy' days such as Christmas and Easter. Once the national railway system was built in Victorian times, everyone could travel and people began taking day trips to the seaside," explained Sir Ralph.

"By the 1960s cars were much cheaper to buy as they were being made in large numbers, so more people had them. This meant that lots of people went on camping holidays in caravans and tents. Holiday camps were popular, too. Our family went camping for years!" said Max.

"When did people start to go **abroad**?" Isabella asked.

> How do they get a holiday in a little package like that?

"People started flying to other countries in large numbers in the 1970s, with 'package holidays', offering travel and accommodation in a package!" said Sir Ralph. "More and more people go every year, especially now there are lots of airlines offering cheap travel."

"That said, have you seen the new campaign encouraging the British to take more holidays at home? I'd better start looking for my old tent!" laughed Max.

Crossword

Fill in the crossword by solving the clues.

Across:

3 Popular holiday in the 1960s
5 You could fly here in the 1970s
6 Fabric houses you can camp in

Down:

1 Popular Victorian holiday
2 They own and run planes
4 In Victorian times, people took these days off work

Ask your grandparents and parents what holidays they remember as a child. You may be surprised!

Did you know?

In Victorian times – and even later – people used to get sent to the coast by their doctors for a 'rest cure'. Sea air was thought to be very healthy, especially for people who had lung and chest diseases such as tuberculosis. In Victorian times, people were also encouraged to bathe in sea water to give them strength.

Where to Now?

Isabella and Sir Ralph are visiting travel agencies, because they want to book a holiday. They have decided to go to Paris during the Easter holidays.

They are comparing the prices of the packages on offer.

"Well, Izzy, at least Easter prices are a bit cheaper than the summer holidays, but not much!" laughed Sir Ralph. "When I went on holiday to India as a student I thought I'd found an amazing bargain, but it turned out it was the rainy season!"

"Why are the prices so different for these two holidays, dad? They're both for the same week," asked Isabella.

"Well, Izzy – the first one has 5 star **accommodation** and the other has 3 stars. 5 star accommodation is smarter and has more facilities, so it's more expensive," said Sir Ralph.

"Meals are included in the first holiday, and so are airport transfers and local taxes. After you've added all those things on to the cost of your holiday, you can see why the first is more expensive."

My choice is Disneyland!

"So, we just need to decide what sort of hotel we want to stay in, what we want to be near to, and how much money we have to spend," said Isabella.

"That's right, Izzy. I'd like to be near to the Louvre or the Orangerie, so we can see lots of wonderful paintings and sculptures…or the Pompidou Centre for some modern art!" said Sir Ralph.

"Hmm. I was thinking more… Disneyland Paris, so I'd better start saving my pocket money!" said Isabella.

Find the words

Find these words in the grid.

facilities	location	airport	taxes	hotel

t	a	x	e	s	e	s	b	v	w	f
h	t	d	e	n	v	g	e	q	a	n
a	o	u	n	t	r	l	s	s	d	o
e	u	t	t	r	o	p	r	i	a	i
r	e	f	e	y	u	l	e	e	t	t
l	e	n	a	l	w	o	r	k	w	a
r	o	o	p	t	c	t	y	i	s	c
f	a	c	i	l	i	t	i	e	s	o
h	e	r	d	u	h	o	o	e	s	l

Top Tips!

Look at prices of holidays in a travel brochure
and see if you can work out why some
holidays are more expensive than others.

Did you know?

Travel agents are experts on travel. They can help you to think about
all the things you need to arrange for your holiday, including health
issues, such as whether you need **vaccinations**, and **insurance** in
case your baggage is lost or stolen, or you need health care whilst you
are on holiday.

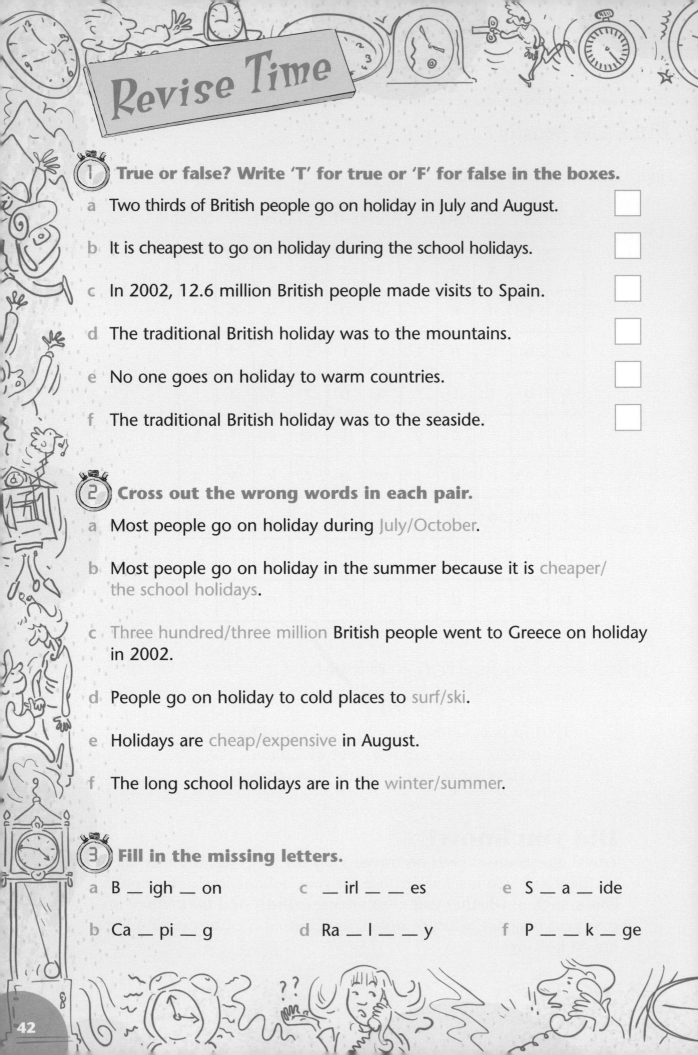

Revise Time

1 **True or false? Write 'T' for true or 'F' for false in the boxes.**

a Two thirds of British people go on holiday in July and August. ☐

b It is cheapest to go on holiday during the school holidays. ☐

c In 2002, 12.6 million British people made visits to Spain. ☐

d The traditional British holiday was to the mountains. ☐

e No one goes on holiday to warm countries. ☐

f The traditional British holiday was to the seaside. ☐

2 **Cross out the wrong words in each pair.**

a Most people go on holiday during July/October.

b Most people go on holiday in the summer because it is cheaper/
the school holidays.

c Three hundred/three million British people went to Greece on holiday
in 2002.

d People go on holiday to cold places to surf/ski.

e Holidays are cheap/expensive in August.

f The long school holidays are in the winter/summer.

3 **Fill in the missing letters.**

a B _ igh _ on   c _ irl _ _ es   e S _ a _ ide

b Ca _ pi _ g   d Ra _ l _ _ y   f P _ _ k _ ge

4 Describe a typical holiday in:

a Victorian times for working people.

_____

_____

b the 1960s – when Sir Ralph was a child.

_____

_____

c the 1970s. _____

_____

5 Circle the correct answer.

a Which hotel has better facilities? 2 star/4 star/5 star

b When is it cheaper to go on holiday?
During the school holidays/when children are at school

c Where would you find the Louvre? London/Paris/New York

d What are travel agents experts in planning? Houses/holidays/schools

e Where is Disneyland found in Europe? Berlin/Madrid/Paris

6 Answer these questions about holidays.

a Name three things a travel agent can help you with.

_____   _____   _____

b List three things that can make a hotel more expensive to stay in.

_____   _____

43

Glossary

abroad to, or in, a foreign country

accommodation the place you stay, such as hotel, when you are on holiday

aerial photograph a photograph taken from the sky or from space

anemometer an instrument that measures wind speed

Antarctic the area around the South Pole

Arctic the area around the North Pole

atlas a book of maps

atmospheric pressure measured by a barometer; the weight of air

barometer an instrument used to measure atmospheric pressure

brochure a magazine providing information – a holiday brochure is an example

camouflage when something is specially coloured so it blends in with the background

canal barges boats that travel on canals; used to be used for moving goods around the country

chamois a small antelope that lives in some areas of Europe, such as in the Alps

communication the sharing or exchange of messages, information and ideas

compact small and solid

compass an instrument used for finding directions

coordinates numbers or letters on a grid to help people find places

equator an imaginary line around the middle of the earth

exchange trip when people from one country visit another country and stay with families; then the people they stayed with make a return visit

globe a ball that shows a map of the earth

graph a diagram that shows the relationship between two or more changing things

grid lines that cross each other to form squares. Grids are used to find points on a map or to make diagrams

grid reference a set of numbers or letters used to find a point on a grid

hemisphere either of two halves of the earth, above and below the equator

hibernate a special deep 'sleep' an animal can use to save energy in the winter

hygrometer an instrument that measures the amount of moisture in the air

insurance money a person pays to insure that, if they have an accident, or lose something valuable, they can claim back money to cover their expenses

key (on a map) a box that shows what the symbols on a map mean

landmark a place or historic building people use to find their way somewhere, e.g. 'turn left at the war memorial' – the memorial would be the landmark

legend box a type of key

location a place or a position

magnetic North the northern direction pointed to by a magnetic needle

migrate to move from one place to another, especially according to the seasons

Ordnance Survey map a detailed map. The whole of the UK is mapped on Ordnance Survey maps

permafrost a permanently frozen soil found under the surface of the ground in Arctic areas

picture atlas a book of maps, usually for children, with pictures relevant to the map

precipitation water falling as rain, snow, sleet, or hail

proportion the correct relation in size between one thing and another

rail network the system of tracks and stations that trains use

rainforest a forest where there is lots of rainfall throughout the year

rain gauge an instrument used for measuring the amount of rainfall

route the way to go to get from one place to another

scale a scale drawing or model is made in proportion so that you can see what size the real object would be

spreadsheet a grid, often made on the computer, which shows figures and information

symbol a picture or thing that represents (stands for) something else

tepee a tent-like house traditionally lived in by native Americans

The Hague a large city in the Netherlands where the Dutch government is found, as well as the International Court of Justice

the Vatican where the Pope (the head of the Catholic Church) lives, in Vatican City

thermometer an instrument for measuring temperature

tundra a flat, treeless area of land found in the Arctic

vaccination an injection or medicine given to a person encouraging their body to make the antibodies needed to fight an illness, should they be exposed to it

weather station a collection of instruments used for recording and predicting the weather

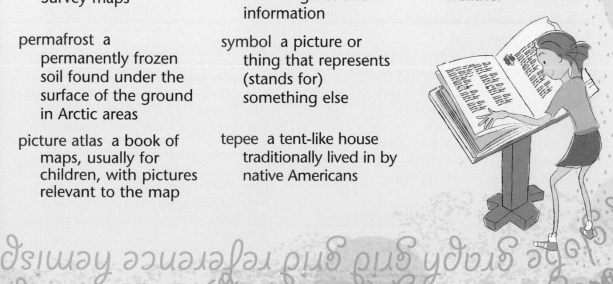

Answers

Page 5

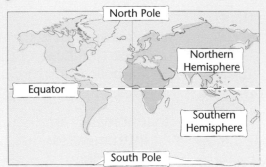

North Pole

Northern Hemisphere

Equator

Southern Hemisphere

South Pole

Page 7

1 Tundra	5 North
2 Seal	6 South
3 Heat	7 Windy
4 Pole	8 Arctic

Page 9

1 To measure temperature
2 To measure rainfall
3 To find wind direction
4 To measure atmospheric pressure
5 To measure wind speed
6 To measure humidity
7 To record readings

Pages 10–11 Revision exercises

Exercise 1

a Equator	d Bottom
b Rainforests	e North Pole
c Northern	f South Pole

Exercise 2

a A round model of the world
b A book of maps
c An imaginary line that runs round the earth
d The half of the globe below the equator
e The half of the globe above the equator
f A damp tropical jungle

Exercise 3

a Penguin	d Permafrost
b Antarctic	e Tundra
c Arctic	f Hibernate

Exercise 4

A variety of answers are appropriate. The following are examples:

a Permafrost is permanently frozen soil
b To keep them warm

c Asia, Europe, and North America
d Arctic fox, ermine
e Blue whale, seal, penguin

Exercise 5

a A way of recording measurements
b How fast the wind is travelling
c A measure of how hot or cold it is
d Warm and damp
e Writing down

Exercise 6

A variety of answers are appropriate. Some examples are:

You could find a rain gauge, which measures the amount of rainfall; a thermometer, which records the temperature; a barometer, which checks atmospheric pressure; an anemometer, which measure the speed of the wind; a hygrometer, which measures humidity.

Page 13

A map with correctly placed items, such as the TGV trains in France, chamois antelopes on the mountains in Switzerland, oranges in Spain, The Hague in Holland and the Vatican and pizza in Italy

Page 15

A correctly drawn map with appropriate landmarks such as churches, trees and shops

Page 17

A suitable email, explaining that emails are quick and easy to write, arrive at their destination virtually instantly and save trees. Photographs can also be attached to them.

Pages 18–19 Revision exercises

Exercise 1

a TGV train	c Leaning tower of Pisa
b Orange	d Chamois

Exercise 2

a Holland	d Italy
b France	e Oranges
c Spain	f Switzerland

Exercise 3

A variety of answers are appropriate. The following are examples:

a A picture that represents a place, and helps us find our way
b The scale lets us know how big something is in real life. (1:10 would mean the real thing is 10x bigger than it appears on the map)
c A place or object that you can look out for to help you find your way
d A way of getting from one place to another
e The correct relation in size between one thing and another
f A place where you can catch a bus or train

Exercise 4

a Proportion
b Journey
c Landmark
d Road
e Route
f Map

Exercise 5

a Air mail
b Internet
c Information
d Email
e Communication
f Photos

Exercise 6

a T
b F
c F
d T
e T
f F

Page 21

1 3.5km
2 2km
3 4km
4 2km
5 5.5km
6 6km

Page 23

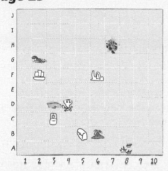

Page 25

1 South
2 East
3 North east
4 South west
5 North
6 North west

Pages 26–27 Revision exercises

Exercise 1

a Symbol
b Legend
c Information
d Scale
e Route
f Distance

Exercise 2

A variety of answers are appropriate. The following are examples:

a A picture that stands for something else

b A legend box is the box which explains what the symbols on the map are used for

c The size of something, found using an instrument such as a ruler or tape measure

d How far away something is or how far it is between points

Exercise 3

a T
b F
c T
d F
e T
f T

Exercise 4

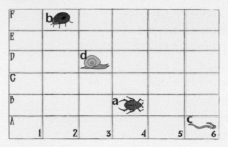

Exercise 5

a Magnet
b One
c Magnetic North
d Direction
e North, east

Exercise 6

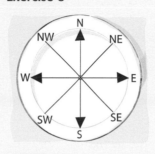

Page 29

1 Garden
2 Castle
3 Campsite
4 Caravan site
5 Nature reserve

Page 31

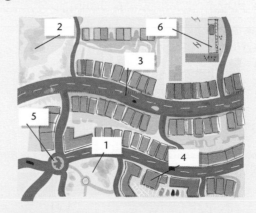

Page 33

Circled: Car, bus, train, plane

Pages 34–35 Revision exercises

Exercise 1

a Something that describes the symbols on a map and helps us to read it

b They give us information quickly

c Nature reserve

d Tiny tepee

e Gardens

f Tiny castle

g Caravan site

Exercise 2

a A picture of a caravan

b A picture of a tepee

c A picture of a flower

d A picture of a castle

e A picture of a duck

Exercise 3

a Aerial

b Photograph

c Shopping centre

d Roundabout

e Houses

Exercise 4

a The sky – in planes or helicopters. They can also be taken from space

b Because the picture is taken from very far away

c A park or field

d A lake or a pond

Exercise 5

a Coaches

b Tube

c Cabs

d Cars

e Network

f Decker

Exercise 6

a 72

b 85

c 16,659

d 100

e 2

Page 37

1 Holiday

2 Summer

3 Winter

4 Brochure

5 School

6 British

Page 39

Across

3 camping

5 abroad

6 tents

Down

1 seaside

2 airlines

4 holy days

Page 41

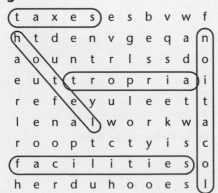

Pages 42–43 Revision exercises

Exercise 1

a T

b F

c T

d F

e F

f T

Exercise 2

The correct sentences are:

a Most people go on holiday during July.

b Most people go on holiday in the summer because it is the school holidays.

c Three million British people went to Greece on holiday in 2002.

d People go on holiday to cold places to ski.

e Holidays are expensive in August.

f The long school holidays are in the summer.

Exercise 3

a Brighton

b Camping

c Airlines

d Railway

e Seaside

f Package

Exercise 4

A variety of answers are possible. Examples are:

a Working people did not go away on holidays as such – they worked all the time. They got 'holy days' off, such as Christmas Day and Easter Day. They took day trips to the seaside on the new railways.

b Seaside holidays in Britain were popular, at resorts such as Brighton, Blackpool, Scarborough and Bournemouth. Children played in the sea and made sandcastles, and watched Punch and Judy shows. People went camping too, in tents and caravans – they went to holiday camps too.

c People started flying overseas in the 1970s, on package holidays. Many people still went on camping and seaside holidays in the 1970s too.

Exercise 5

a 5 star

b when children are at school

c Paris

d Holidays

e Paris

Exercise 6

a Accommodation, flights, meals, health requirements, insurance

b Facilities, location, time of year